Key Words of the English language

Some words in our language are used much more frequently than others. Three hundred of the most frequently used words make up about three-quarters of the total number of words used in juvenile reading. The very common words have been called Key Words, and reading skill is accelerated if these important words are learned early.

This first dictionary introduces ninety two Key Words in pictorial form, and the words chosen lend themselves to easy, unambiguous illustration.
Sixty eight nouns are presented, thirty two appearing again in the plural form. Eleven verbs in everyday use are included, also the most commonly used numbers and colours.

© LADYBIRD BOOKS LTD MCMLXXX

A First Ladybird Key Words
Picture Dictionary

by J McNALLY

illustrations by
HURLSTON DESIGN LTD

bird

Jessica Harrell

Ladybird Books Loughborough

apple

apples

baby

bag

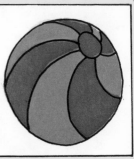

ball

balls

bed

bird

birds

blue

black

boat

boats

book

books

box

boys

boy

bus

cake

cakes

cap

caps

car

cars

cats

cat

chair **chairs**

COW

COWS

children

cup

cups

dog

dogs

doll

dolls

door

down

**draw
drawing**

drink
drinking

eat
eating

egg

eggs

farm

fire

first

fish

five

5

flower

flowers

four

4

girl

girls

green

hand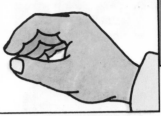

hands

hat

hats

head

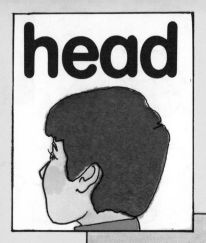

hill

horse

 **horses**

house

houses

ink

jam

jump
jumping

king

last

letter

letters

letters

man

men

milk

money

nail

1 one

open

peg

pegs

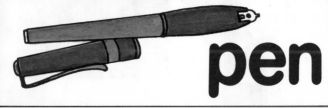

pen

pens

pencil

pencils

picture

play
playing

policeman

pull

push

queen

rabbit

rain

read
reading

red

road

room

run

school

sea

seat

shop

shops

sing
singing

street

sun

sweets

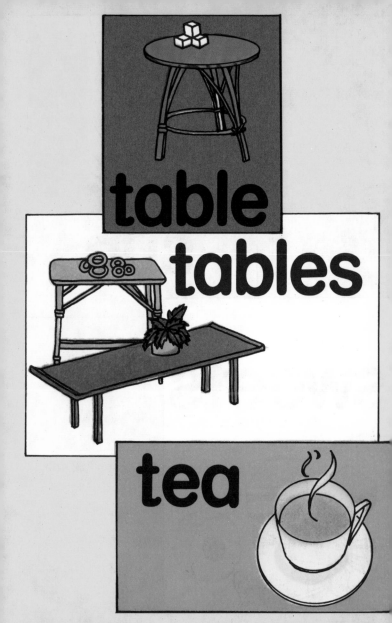

table

tables

tea

3 ∴

three

toy

toys

train

tree

trees

2
two

up

van

water

white

window

woman

women

write

yellow

zoo

List of words in this dictionary

apple
apples

---

baby
bag
ball
balls
bed
bird
birds
black
blue
boat
boats
book
books
box
boy
boys
bus

---

cake
cakes
cap

caps
car
cars
cat
cats
chair
chairs
children
cow
cows
cup
cups

---

dog
dogs
doll
dolls
door
down
draw
drawing
drink
drinking

---

eat

eating
egg
eggs

---

farm
fire
first
fish
five
flower
flowers
four

---

girl
girls
green

---

hand
hands
hat
hats
head
hill
horse
horses